D1237433

My First Animal Library

Aardvarks

by Penelope S. Nelson

Bullfrog Books

Ideas for Parents and Teachers

Bullfrog Books let children practice reading informational text at the earliest reading levels. Repetition, familiar words, and photo labels support early readers.

Before Reading

• Discuss the cover photo. What does it tell them?

• Look at the picture glossary together. Read and discuss the words.

Read the Book

• "Walk" through the book and look at the photos. Let the child ask questions. Point out the photo labels.

• Read the book to the child, or have him or her read independently.

After Reading

• Prompt the child to think more. Ask: Have you heard about aardvarks before reading this book? What more would you like to learn about them after reading it?

Bullfrog Books are published by Jump!
5357 Penn Avenue South
Minneapolis, MN 55419
www.jumplibrary.com

Library of Congress Cataloging-in-Publication Data

Names: Nelson, Penelope, 1994– author.
Title: Aardvarks / by Penelope S. Nelson.
Description: Bullfrog books edition.
Minneapolis, MN : Jump!, Inc., [2020]
Series: My first animal library
Audience: Age 5–8. | Audience: K to Grade 3.
Includes index.
Identifiers: LCCN 2018036977 (print)
LCCN 2018039027 (ebook)
ISBN 9781641285513 (ebook)
ISBN 9781641285506 (hardcover : alk. paper)
Subjects: LCSH: Aardvark—Juvenile literature.
Classification: LCC QL737.T8 (ebook)
LCC QL737.T8 N45 2019 (print)
DDC 599.3/1—dc23
LC record available at https://lccn.loc.gov/2018036977

Editor: Jenna Trnka
Designer: Jenna Casura

Photo Credits: Eric Isselee/Shutterstock, cover, 8, 12; GlobalP/iStock, 1, 3, 22, 24; Paul Wishart/Shutterstock, 4; Nigel Dennis/Age Fotostock, 5, 23tr; Mint Images - Frans Lanting/Getty, 6–7; NHPA/SuperStock, 9; Gael Le Roc'h/Biosphoto, 10–11, 12–13, 23bl; Asholove/Shutterstock, 14–15, 23br; Attila JANDI/Shutterstock, 16, 23tl; Aaron Amat/Shutterstock, 17; charliemarcos/iStock, 18–19; Martin Harvey/Cultura Limited/SuperStock, 20–21.

Printed in the United States of America at Corporate Graphics in North Mankato, Minnesota.

Table of Contents

Diggers

An aardvark sleeps during the day.

The sun sets.

It is dusk.

The aardvark wakes up.

snout

It sniffs for food.

With what?

Its snout!

It has long claws.

claw

For what?
Digging!

9

It digs and eats
at night.

It finds a mound.

Its tongue is long.

And sticky.

Why?

To catch food.

tongue

12

mound

termite

What does it catch?

Termites.

Yum!

burrow

Aardvarks dig burrows.
They sleep in them.

hyena

And hide
in them.
From what?
Hyenas. Lions.

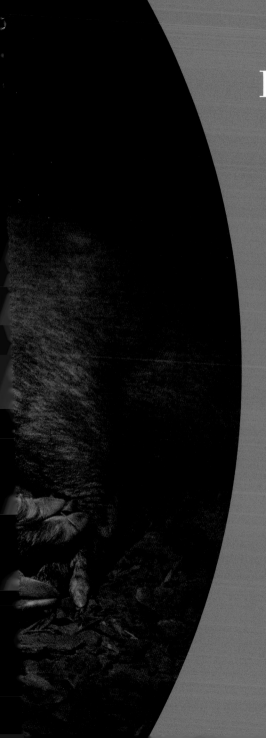

Babies are born here.

They are safe.

They stay for weeks.

They grow up!
They dig their
own burrows.

Parts of an Aardvark

ears
Aardvarks' ears are long and listen for danger.

hair
Aardvarks are lightly covered in hair.

tail
Aardvarks have long, heavy tails.

eyes
Aardvarks have small eyes and cannot see well.

snout
Aardvarks have long snouts to help them smell food.

claws
Aardvarks have large claws that help them dig quickly.

Picture Glossary

burrows
Holes or tunnels in the ground where animals live.

dusk
The time of day after the sun sets and it starts getting dark.

mound
A hill or pile of something.

termites
Ant-like insects that eat wood.

Index

To Learn More

Finding more information is as easy as 1, 2, 3.

❶ Go to www.factsurfer.com

❷ Enter "aardvarks" into the search box.

❸ Click the "Surf" button to see a list of websites.